My First Book for
Listening and Speaking

我的第一本
英语听说
入门书 2

丁洁◎著

北京联合出版公司

如何使用这本书

❶ 教与学的几个原则

（1）把培养听说和全方位能力结为整体。绝不允许课前预习，而要通过我们设定的每个教学环节，在使学生获得听说能力的同时，提高全方位的能力。

（2）心系全班，切实做到把学和用结为整体。老师应随教学实践对学生的了解为每个学生建档。其内容包括家庭环境、个人的性格特长和爱好，以及学习英语的许多变化进步的细节，以便结合实际，教活所学的语言内容。为此，对于人数过多的班级组，建课后学习小组是必要的，这样做有利于更好地了解学生，有针对性地不断树立变后进为先进的典型，有利于培养干部并争创集体荣誉。

（3）老师配合教学的手势、眼神、表情和动作务必准确明白。这样做有利于学生理解、仿效，使学生们全身心动起来。还可用简单的指向方式，便捷又具体地组织师生间的多角提问。总之，利用课堂四十分钟的分分秒秒，营造全班教学有序、思维敏捷、积极主动、节奏欢快的学习氛围。

（4）牢记英语课上唱英语歌的目的是通过节奏给大脑的刺激，使思维与语言的固有频率引起共振，从而促使记忆。但唱好歌的前提必须是能正确地吐词发音，满足于哼唱小曲般的滥唱只能浪费课时，而无助于获得听说能力。全书依据教学的需要，提供了可供听说、戏耍等不同要求的十多首英语歌曲。如能结合学过的内容，在学会听说的基础上再选唱作者撰写的《101首英语歌曲大家唱》中的有关曲目，定能事半功倍地培养出一批能听说、会演唱，有扎实基本功的英语人才。

❷ 教学的具体步骤和方法

（1）看。在上每一课新书时，先让学生认真仔细地观看有关图像，以便对画面呈现的形象有初步的直觉反映。在刚接触本教材时，可允许学生用母语简述对画面的第一印象，经相互启发来抓住重点。老师绝对不能逐词逐句汉英对译。大约用一两分钟即可。

（2）看听。边看图像、边听录音两三遍。一般占时三四分钟。起始阶段，放听第一遍录音时，应首先配合声音搞清楚图像中出现的男女学生是谁和谁在交谈。他们是如何以彼此的英文名字相称呼的。在放听第二遍录音时，使学习者既形象又直接地通过画面理解声音的意思，以保证声音和图像的协调作用。达到初步整体感知语音、语调、节奏等语句中大约百分之三十的内容。必要时再放听第三遍录音，其目的是配合音和像的紧密结合，了解本课书要学习的内容重点。

(3) 看听说演示。演示是课堂教学中最为重要的环节，是决定教学成败的关键。一般每课书都需用25到30分钟来组织教学。按课文逐步演示练习，演示结束后，应再完整地放听全课录音，以加深印象。

在演示过程中，首先应顺应语言的逻辑，针对新课对话中的新单词、习惯用语、主题内容、语言结构等特点，抓住重点、分层次地用由浅入深、以旧带新等方式，逐个进行边推理、边学习、边记忆的讲练演示，可根据需要穿插图像呈现的情景，使学生凭借图像，让语言和意义联系起来。但用图像的目的在于将来摈弃图像，使语言和意义直接联系。因此，必须将画面中要说明的某个词或短语的有关内容和实际中的人和物相互联系，使学生在老师迅速变换的内容方式提问中说出尽可能多、尽可能新、尽可能不重复的话。在交谈的实践中，还应有目的地配合听录音，加深学习者注意语音语调和表情达意的关系，从而更进一步理解，达到基本掌握某个新单词的发音、意义和在语句中相应的功能。使学生听到有关的"音"，就能直接感知其语言的涵义。

(4) 听说演唱。用时约五六分钟。演示结束，由老师根据演示过程中对学生的了解，及时组织表演，反馈学习掌握的情况。为让每个学生都能因各自展现的才华受到肯定而享受到学习的乐趣，还应允许有的学生在课后再作准备，自行分配角色，于第二天上课时进行表演。重视平时的表演，将其作为学期重要的考核成绩。期末考试表演的内容方式可由师生共同议定。既为老师近距离了解学生、进行具体指导创造机会，又能增进师生间的互信，有效发挥学生综合运用语言的能力和组织能力。

丁洁于2012年8月

目 录

Contens

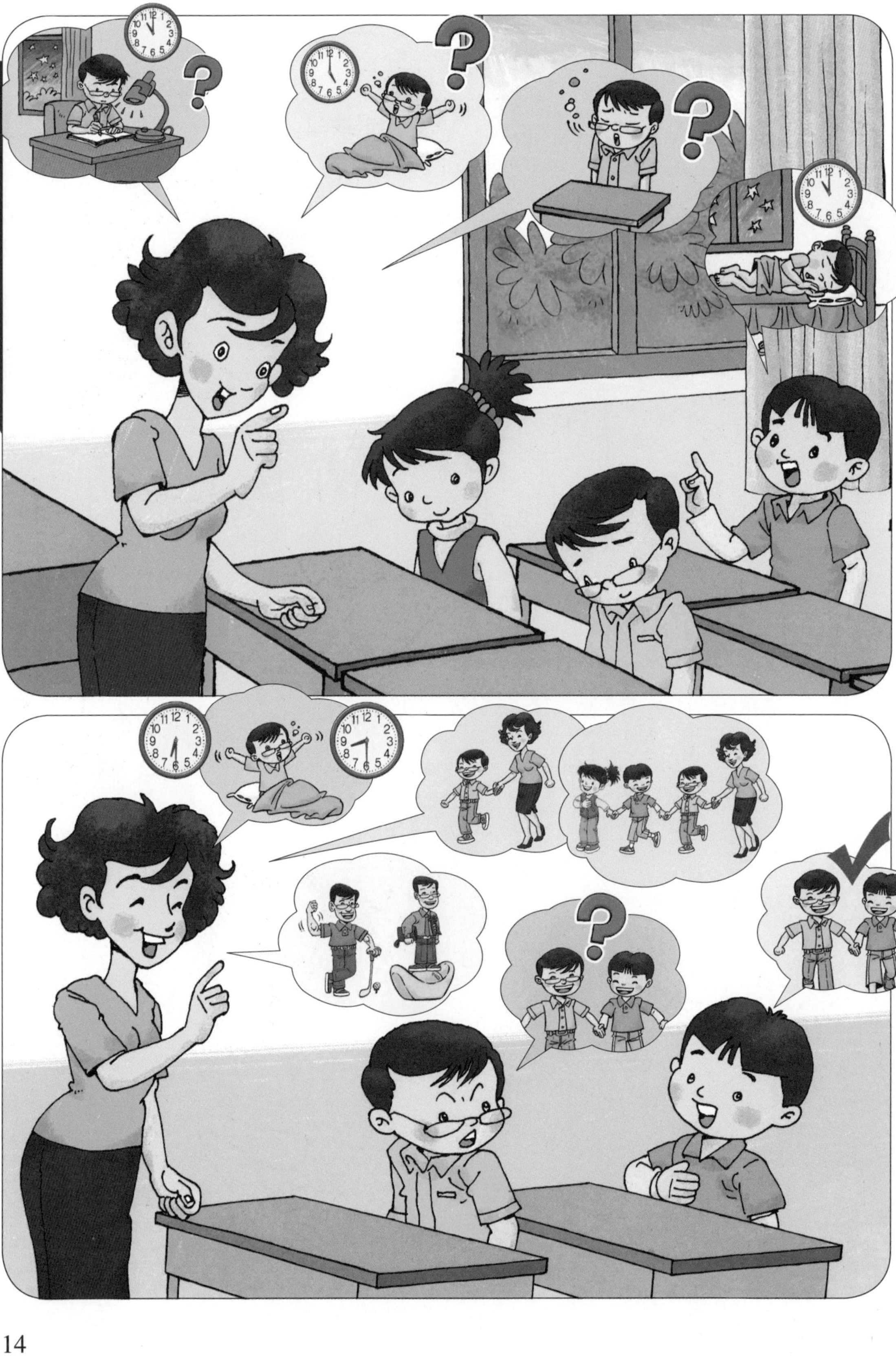

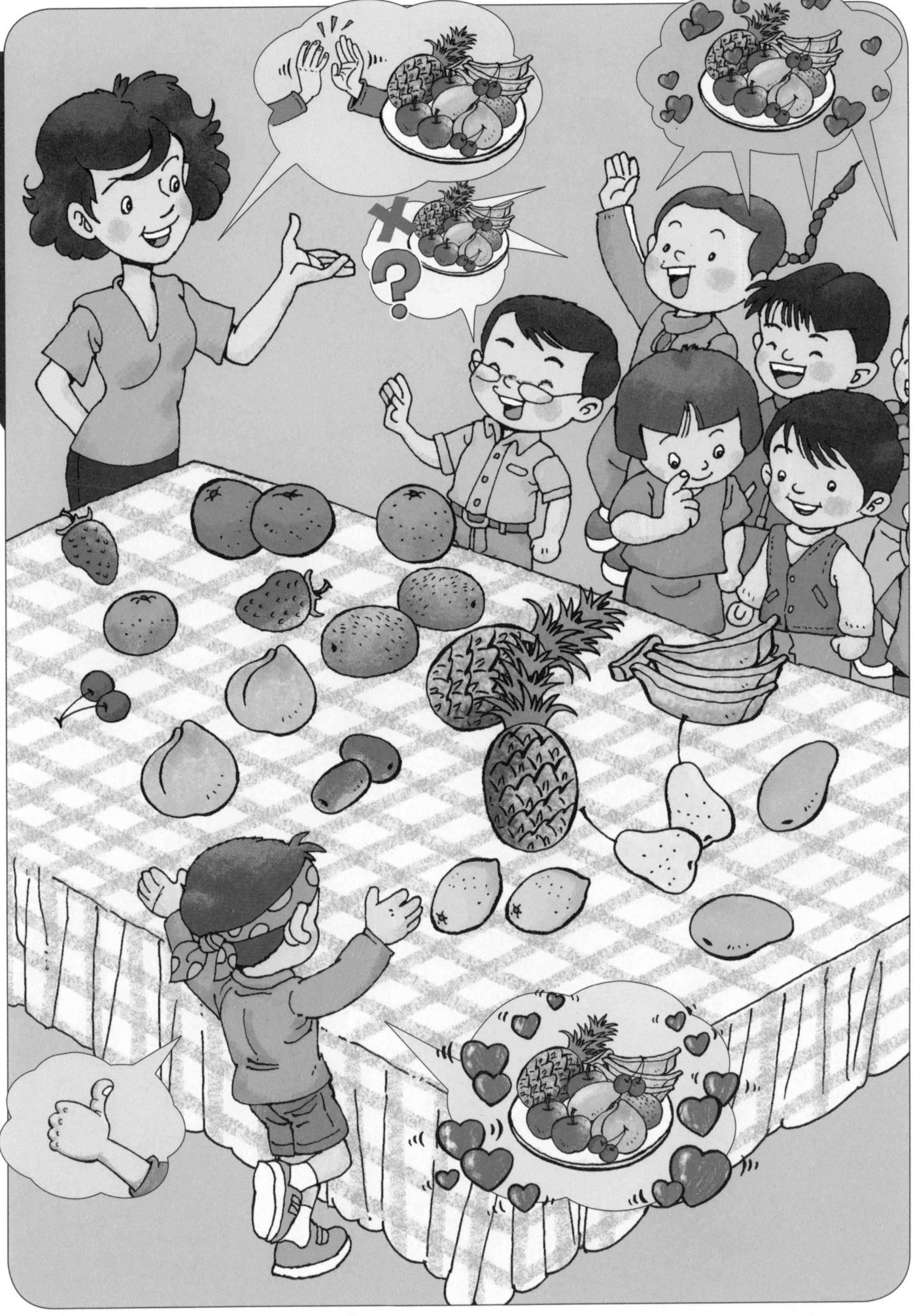

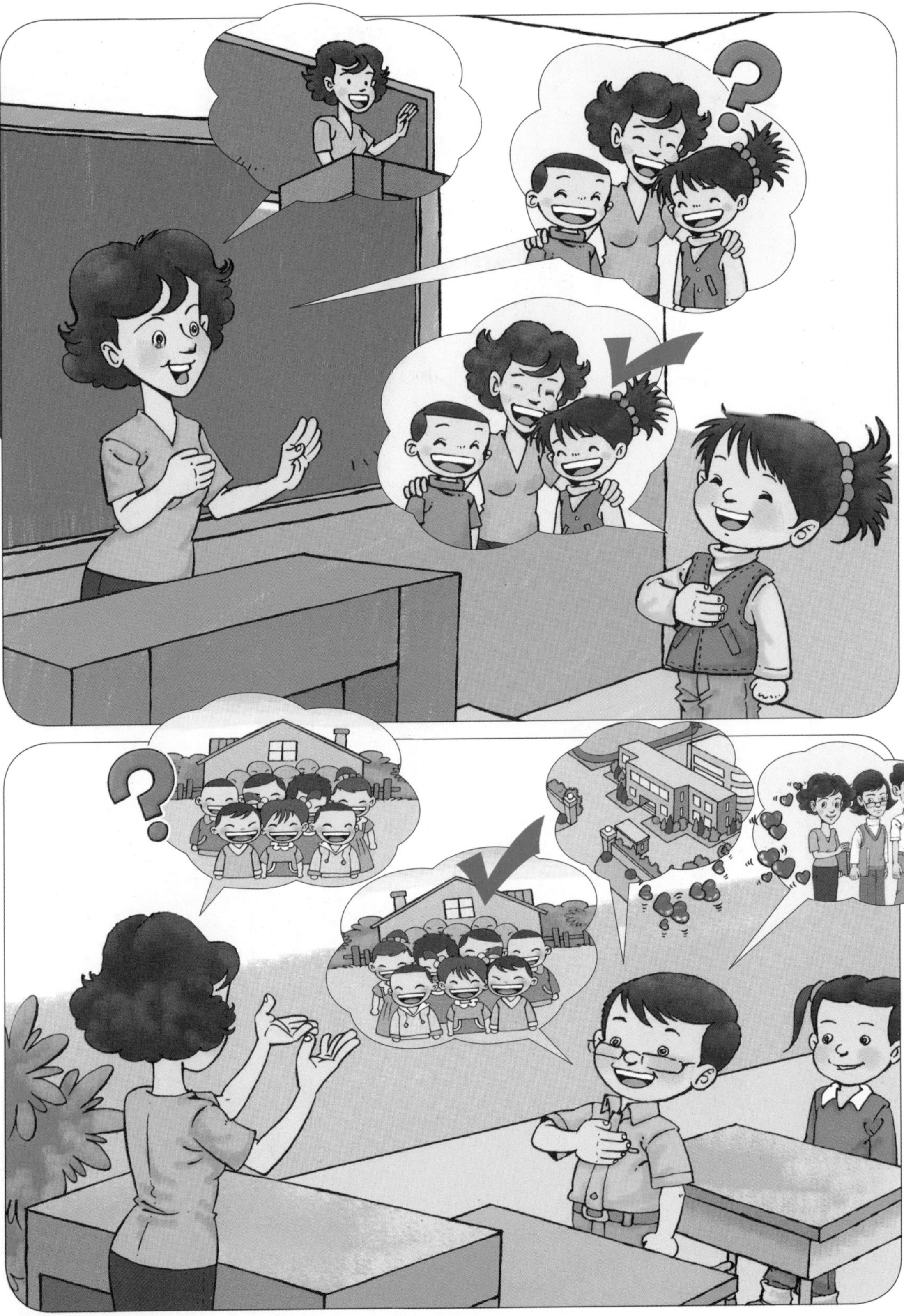

30

44

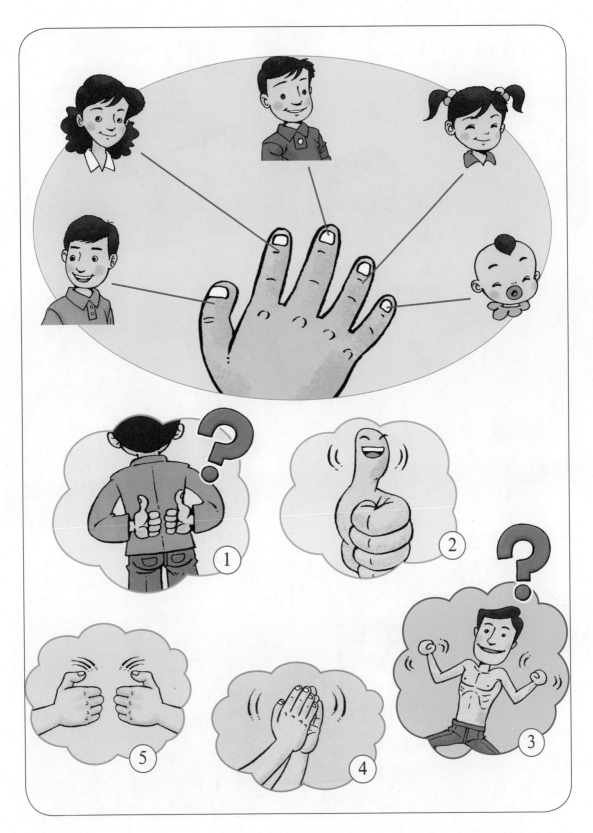

50

58

66

68

附　录

Unit 1 Keep in Shape
Lesson 1 Exercise

Ms. Ding: Hi everybody. How are you doing today?

All: Super great. We miss you so much, Ms. Ding. How are you?

Ms. Ding: Very well, thank you. I miss you all too. Today is the first day of the new semester. Let's start by learning a song "Exercise".

Steve: Exercise?

Ms. Ding: Yes, exercise. Listen please.
(Singing: Exercise)
Exercise. Exercise. Keep doing exercise. Exercise your mind. Exercise your body. Exercise. Exercise. Keep doing exercise. Exercise your body and mind. Exercise day by day.

Ms. Ding: Now let's exercise our body and mind, and do it everyday.

All: (Singing while doing exercise)

Lesson 2 Do Eye Exercise

Isaac: Now it's time to do eye exercise. Start, please.
One, two, three, four, five, six, seven, eight; Two, two, three, four, five, six, seven, eight; Three, two, three, four, five, six, seven, eight; Four, two, three, four, five, six, seven, eight;
Please stop. Would you please do it well? Ok. Now let's start it over, please.

Lesson 3 Our Daily Exercise

Isaac: Exercise, exercise. What is our daily exercise?

Ulysses: How about running in the morning?

Isaac: Running? Oh, yes. Let's go running every morning.

All: Good. We like running. Let's go for a run now.

Isaac: Not now. We will start tomorrow morning.

Helen: Running in the morning does not work for me. I like walking. Let's walk in the evening.

Amy: A good idea. We girls like walking. Let's walk after school.

Isaac: Well, do what you like, walking, jumping rope, or playing ball. Just keep doing exercise every day.

Steve: Let's exercise our mind too. Let's keep learning everyday.

Lesson 4 Mr. Rooster Is Crowing

Alarm clock: Cock-a –doodle-do. Good morning. It's six, time to get up, please.
(Sound of saying)
Go to bed late, stay very small.
Go to bed early, grow very tall.

Tom: Listen. It's six in the morning. Time to get up, daddy.

Mrs. Liu: Yes. It's time for you to rise.

Mr. Liu: What? Is it time for me to get up? Oh, no! It's too early for me to get up.

Mrs. Liu: You promised Tom to go to the zoo today. So you have to get up right now.

Tom: Yes, daddy, let's go to the zoo. Thank you, mom.

Mr. Liu: All right. A promise is a promise. Let me get up and be ready for the zoo.

I'm ready now. Let's go to the zoo together.

Lesson 5 Have a Good Sleep

Ms. Ding: You look tired and sleepy, Steve. Why? Do you get up very early everyday?

Steve: (No answer)

Ms. Ding: Does Steve stay up very late everyday?

James: Yes, he does. Sometimes he goes to bed very late.

Steve: Hey, James! Are you my friend?

James: Yes. I am your good friend.

Ms. Ding: James is your good friend. We are all your good friends. Now listen to this old saying.

Early to bed and early to rise .
Make a man healthy, wealthy and wise.

Ms. Ding: So everybody needs a good sleep everyday.

Have a good sleep, to be strong.
Have a good sleep, to grow fast.
Have a good sleep, to stay healthy.
Have a good sleep, to feel great.

Steve: From now on, I'll go to bed early everyday. Thank you, James. You are my good friend. Thank you, Ms. Ding, and thank you all.

Isaac: Everybody wants to be strong and healthy.

All: So let's have a good sleep everyday.

Lesson 6 Lazy Helen

Ms. Ding: Here is a doll. Her name is Helen. Now listen to a new song before we play house.
(Singing)
Lazy, lazy, lazy Helen, will you, will you, will you get up, please?

No, no, Mama. I won't get up. I will, I will, I will sleep all day.

Ms. Ding: Let's play house now. Who wants to be that Helen? And who wants to be her mama or her papa?

Helen: I will be Helen and also her mama. (Acting out the dialogue)

Mama: Helen, get up now. It is late in the morning.

Helen: Sorry, mama. I won't get up. I will sleep all day.

Mama: Don't be lazy, Helen. Get up or you will be late for school.

Helen: Late for school? Oh, no. I don't want to be late for school. I have to get up right now. I am not lazy, Mama.

All: Wonderful! You act very well, Helen!

Helen: Thank you.

Lesson 7 Good Food

David: Look! There is a lot of food in here. I'm hungry.

Vicky: I'm hungry too. Good! There is no junk food but good food here.

David: Junk food? What is junk food? What is good food?

Vicky: French fries and potato chips are junk food. They do no good to our body. Do you like the whole wheat bread?

David: No, I don't like the whole wheat bread. It tastes bad.

Vicky: But whole wheat bread or whole grain bread is good food. We eat good food to be healthy.

David: I see. Good food is healthy food.

Vicky: You are very smart. We are what we eat.

David: From now on, I'll try to eat whole wheat bread.

Lesson 8 Fish or Meat

Helen: I like fish. It tastes good. Do you like fish?

Amy: Yes, I do. I like fish, but I don't like meat. Does Tom like fish?

Ulysses: No, he doesn't. He doesn't like fish. He is a big meat eater. He likes meat.

Isaac: Let me sing a song about fish and meat.
Do you like fish? Do you like fish? Yes, I do. Yes, I do. I don't like meat, I don't like meat. I like fish. I like fish.
Does he like fish? Does he like fish? No, he doesn't. No, he doesn't. He doesn't like fish. He doesn't like fish. He likes meat. He likes meat.

Isaac: Now, let's sing together.

Lesson 9 Vegetables

Ms. Ding: Vegetables are good for us. I like peppers, cucumbers, cauliflowers, and tomatoes.

Vicky: Ms. Ding likes peppers, cucumbers, cauliflowers, and tomatoes. We like peppers, cucumbers, cauliflowers, and tomatoes, too.

Ms. Ding: I like onions, bitter melons and carrots.

Ulysses: Yuck! I don't like carrots. I don't like onions, I don't….

Steve: What do you like then? Do you know vegetables are good for us?

James: Do you like onions, Steve?

Steve: Yes, I do, I like the onion's strong taste.

Tom: Do you like bitter melons then?

Steve: Yes, I do. I like the taste of bitter melons.

Ms. Ding: Well, do you like carrots?

All: Yes, we do. We all like carrots except Ulysses.

Lesson 10 Fruit Party (1)

Ms. Ding: Hello, friends. Come on in, please. Welcome to our fruit party.

Tom: Wow, so many fruits. I like fruits.

All: Who doesn't? We all like fruits.

Ms. Ding: Before we start, let's first sing a song "Yummy" together.
(Singing: Fruits)
Yummy, yummy, oranges are juicy.
Yummy, yummy, grapefruits are juicy.
Yummy, yummy, cherries are good to eat.
Yummy, yummy, strawberries are sweet.
Yummy, yummy, peaches are juicy.
Yummy, yummy, kiwis are juicy.
Yummy, yummy, dates are good to eat.
Yummy, yummy, pineapples are sweet.
Yummy, yummy, lemons are juicy.
Yummy, yummy, pears are juicy.
Yummy, yummy, mangos are good to eat.
Yummy, yummy, bananas are sweet.

Lesson 11 Fruit Party (2)

Ms. Ding: All kinds of fruits are good for health. Now name the one you like best.

Amy: Oranges, peaches, pears, grapefruits, kiwis, and lemons are all very juicy. But I like oranges best.

Hope: Dates, bananas, cherries, strawberries, and pineapples are all very sweet. But I like strawberries best of all.

James: Sweet mangos are my first choice.

Steve: Watermelon is juicy, sweet and good to eat. I like watermelons.

Tony: My first pick is grapes. Grapes are good for health.

Lesson 12 Dairy Food

Ms. Ding: Do you drink milk everyday?

Tom: Yes, I do. I like milk very much.

Amy: I drink milk in the morning. I drink milk in the evening before bed.

Tony: Me too. I also like ice-cream, butter, cheese and yogurt very much. As you see, I'm tall and very strong.

Tom: I'm strong too.

Unit 2 Family Love

Lesson 1 We Are a Big Happy Family

Ms. Ding: I am your teacher. Am I your friend too?

Hope: Yes, you are. You are our best friend. We are good friends.

Ms. Ding: Are we a big happy family?

Steve: Yeah, we are a big happy family. We love our school and our teachers.

Ms. Ding: Do you help each other like brothers and sisters?

Tom: Sure, we do. We help each other like brothers and sisters.

All: The school is like a big family. We are like brothers and sisters.

Lesson 2 We Are Twins

Kate: He is my twin brother. I love him.

Kent: She is my twin sister. I love her.

Kate: I love you. You love me.

Kent: We love each other.

Kate: I help you. You help me.

Kent: We help each other.

Kate: We are twins.

Kent: We're twin brother and sister.

Lesson 3 Family Love

Ms. Ding: Here's a song about family love. Listen.

(Singing: Family Love)

Father and mother love their son and daughter.
Son and daughter love their father and mother.
Brother and sister, sister and brother, love, love, love, love, love each other.

Ms. Ding: Is Kate your sister, Kent?

Kent: Yes, she is my twin sister.

Ms. Ding: Kent and Kate are twins. They are twin brother and sister. What is your family name, Kent?

Kent: My family name is Wang.

Ms. Ding: Who is their father?

Ulysses: Mr. Wang is their father.

Ms. Ding: Mrs. Wang is their mother. Who is Mr. and Mrs. Wang's son?

Kent: I am.

Tom: Kent is their son.

Eva: Kate is their daughter.

Ms. Ding: Do Kent and Kate love their father and mother?

Steve: Yes, they do. They love their father and mother.

Ms. Ding: Do Mr. and Mrs. Wang love their son and daughter?

Isaac: Yes, they love their son and daughter very much.

Ms. Ding: Now let's sing the song "Family Love".

All: Ok, let's sing. (Singing)

Lesson 4 A Great Big Hug

Helen: Welcome home, mom. I love you and I miss you. How are you?

Ms. An: I am fine. I am very glad to be home with you. You know I miss you a lot. Come here, Helen, give me a hug and a kiss.

Helen: Ok, here is my great hug and kiss. Can I sing you a song?
I love you, you love me. We are a

happy family.
With a great, great big hug, and a kiss from me to you.
With a great, great big hug, and a kiss from me to you.
We are a happy family. We are a happy family.

Lesson 5 What Is a Mother?

Ms. Ding: What is a mother?
Amy: A mother is a teacher.
Steve: A mother is a friend.
Isaac: A mother is love.
Ms. Ding: Yes. A mother is love, the deepest love and the endless love. No friendship, no love is like that of the mother's.

Lesson 6 Happy Mother's Day

(Sound of reading)
The second Sunday of May is Mother's Day.
Helen: Today is Mother's Day. Happy Mother's Day. You are a wonderful mom. I love you so much. These flowers are for you.
Ms. An: Oh, they are beautiful flowers. Thank you. I love you too. Come and give me a hug!

Lesson 7 Happy Children's Day

Ms. Ding: Today is June 1st. It is your day. Let's sing together the song "Happy Children's Day".
All: *Happy, happy, happy Children's Day, happy Children's Day.*
Happy, happy, happy Children's Day. This song is for us all.
We are very happy today.
Ms. Ding: I hope you will be happy, strong and healthy forever.

Hope: Thank you, Ms. Ding.
Ms. Ding: My pleasure.

Lesson 8 What Is a Father?

Ms. Ding: What is a father?
Tony: A father is a teacher and a friend.
Vicky: A father is love. A father is sunshine.
Adam: I love my father. My father loves me.
Jane: My father is my sunshine. He helps me a lot. He plays with me and he makes me happy.

Lesson 9 Happy Father's Day

(Sound of reading)
The third Sunday in June is Father's Day.
Steve: Today is Father's Day. "Happy Father's Day", daddy. I have something for you.
Mr. Zhang: For me? What is it?
Steve: See, a book. Do you like it?
Mr. Zhang: Oh yes, I do. I like the book. Thank you.

Lesson 10 "Where" Song

Ms. An: Where are you, Helen? Where is our daughter? Where is she?
Mr. Wei: She is singing in the study. Listen.
(1) Where is my father? Where is my father?
Here I am. Here I am.
How are you today, sir? Very well, thank you.
Have a good day. Have a good day.
(2) (mother, mom)
(3) (brother, sir)
(4) (sister, Miss)
(5) (baby, baby)

Lesson 11 My Family and Me

Kent: My first name is Kent. My family name is Wang. I am six years old. I have a twin sister. Her name is Kate. This is my father. His name is Eric Wang. This is my mother. Her name is Julia Zhang. My father is a teacher. He teaches English. My mother is a teacher too. She teaches Chinese.

Lesson 12 A Family Tree

Ms. Ding: Some families are big, and some families are small. People in a family live together, work together, and play together.

Amy: My father's mother is my grandma. She lives with us. We love her very much.

Tony: My mother's father is my grandpa. He lives with my aunt.

Eva: My father's little brother is my uncle. We live together and play together.

Ms. Ding: Your grandfathers and grandmothers have their parents. This is called a family tree because of its endless branches.

Kent: My family is not big. I live with my father, mother and sister. But my parents have their parents, and their parents' parents. It goes on and on and on. How fun!

Unit 3 Colors
Lesson 1 What Color Do You See?

Ms. Ding: What color do you see in the picture No. 1?

Jane: I see blue, the color of the blue sky and the blue sea. What color do you see in this picture?

James: I see red, yellow and green; the red light, the yellow light and the green light. And I see a red pepper, a yellow pepper, and a green pepper.

Eva: Cucumbers are green. Tomatoes are red.

Steve: I see red and green. Some grapes are red. Some grapes are green.

Vicky: I see red, yellow and green too. Cherries are red. Bananas are yellow. Bitter melons are green.

Ms. Ding: Well done. You are very smart. What color do you see in the picture No. 3?

Tom: Let me see. What color are the oranges? Oh, oranges are orange. I see orange. Am I right?

Ms. Ding: Yes, you are right. You are very bright. Good job.

Lesson 2 The Parade of Colors

Ms. Ding: Now we are the parade of colors. Let's sing and march on.

All: Ok. Let's sing.
Red, green, pink, brown, yellow, purple, white and black.
Red, green, pink, brown, yellow, purple, white and black.
Red, green, pink, brown, yellow, purple, white and black.
We all go marching on.
Green, grey, blue, brown, yellow and white.
Green, grey, blue, brown, yellow and white.
Green, grey, blue, brown, yellow and white.
We all go marching on.

Lesson 3 What Color Do You Like Best?

Ms. Ding: What color do you see, Ida?

Ida: I see white. I see green. I see red and I see black. I see brown. I see grey. I see pink and blue.

Ms. Ding: What color do you like best? What color do you like best?

Judy: I like yellow. She likes purple. We like purple and yellow best.

Ms. Ding: Come on, everybody. Pick a color you like best. As for me, I like yellow best. I pick the yellow one.

Ida: I like white best. I pick the white one.

Adam: I like black best. I pick the black one.

Steve: I like green best. I pick the green one.

Helen: I like red best. I pick the red one.

Amy: I like gray best. I pick the gray one.

Ms. Ding: Who likes brown? Do you like brown, Howard?

Howard: Yes, I do. I like brown best. Let me pick the brown one.

Vicky: I like pink best. I take the pink one.

Shirley: I like purple best. I pick the purple one.

Ulysses: I like blue best. I take the blue one.

Lesson 4 What Color Are Your Shoes?

Ms. Ding: Now listen to the words of the "Color Song".

(Singing)

I see white. I see green. I see red and I see black.
I see brown. I see gray. I see pink and blue.
What color are your shoes? What color are your shoes?
One is green. One is gray. They are green and gray.

Ms. Ding: What color are the little boy's shoes?

Eva: They are green.

Ms. Ding: Sorry. You are wrong.

Amy: They are gray.

Ms. Ding: Sorry. You are wrong too, Amy.

Steve: I know. One is green and one is gray. They are green and gray.

Ms. Ding: You are right and you are very smart. Now learn to sing this song.

Lesson 5 What Color Is/Are…?

Ms. Ding: Here are some pens. Please ask each other questions about their colors.

Tony: What color is the pen?

Helen: It is red and white.

Tom: What color are these two pens?

Adam: They are black.

Tom: I like this one. What color is this pen? What color is it?

Amy: It has many colors: purple, red, yellow, and blue.

Steve: Are they grey?

James: No, they are not grey. They are green.

Ms. Ding: Yes, both are green. One is light green. One is dark green.

Lesson 6 Colors of Eyes and Hair

Ms. Ding: What color is your hair? Is it black or brown?

Amy: My hair is black. It is black hair.

Ms. Ding: What color is her hair?

Hope: Her hair is brown. It is brown hair. My hair is black.

Ms. Ding: What color are Tom's eyes? Are they brown, black or blue?

James: They are brown.

Ms. Ding: My eyes are brown too. See.

Vicky: Oh, yes. Your eyes are brown.

Helen: They are beautiful brown eyes.

Ms. Ding: Thank you.

Lesson 7 The Colorful Rainbow

Ms. Ding: Now look up in the sky. Can you see the beautiful rainbow? It is so colorful: red, orange, yellow, green, blue, indigo and purple. Seven colors!

All: Oh, yes, seven colors in all: red, orange, yellow, green, blue, indigo, and purple.

Ms. Ding: Here is a song of the rainbow. Let's try to sing it together.

Red, orange, yellow, green, blue, indigo, and purple.
Red, orange, yellow, green, blue, indigo, and purple.
Red, orange, yellow, green, blue, indigo, and purple.
The seven colors in the rainbow. How beautiful!

Lesson 8 Let's Color

Ms. Ding: What's the color of the monkey?

James: It is brown.

Ms. Ding: Now, can you color a monkey picture?

Tom: Yes, I can. I can color the monkey brown. See. It is a brown monkey.

Ms. Ding: Good! Here are some pictures of a bear, a bird, a dog and a cat.

All: Oh, a bear, a bird, a dog and a cat.

Ms. Ding: Now take a picture and color it the way you like.

All: Ok.

Tony: Let me take the bear.

Ulysses: I will take the bird.

Ida: I will pick the dog.

Adam: Cat for me.

Lesson 9 Painting

Tony: What's the color of the bear? Is it white, black or brown?

Vicky: It is brown. It is a brown bear.

Ulysses: Now guess. What's the color of the bird?

Jane: It is purple.

Ulysses: No, it isn't purple. Guess again.

Jane: It is blue. It is a blue bird. Am I right?

Ulysses: You are right and you are smart.

Ida: What's the color of the dog? Is it black or white?

Eva: It is white. It is a white dog.

Ida: I like white best. I like my white dog.

Adam: What's the color of my cat?

Steve: It is black. It is a black cat.

Adam: Yeah. It is a beautiful black cat. I like my cat very much.

Lesson 10 I Like Painting

Ms. Ding: You all like painting. Now look, I have a coloring book. It has a horse, a frog, a duck and a parrot. Take one and paint the color you like.

Helen: I take the horse.

Steve: I take the frog.

Shirley: I take the parrot.

Judy: I take the duck.

Ms. Ding: Now paint it the color you like.

Helen: I like red best. Here is my horse, a red horse.

Hope: Steve likes green best.

Steve: Yes, I like green best. Here is my green frog.

Shirley: I like purple best. So this is my purple parrot.

Judy: Ms. Ding and I like yellow. So this is our beautiful little yellow duck.

Lesson 11 A Guessing Game

Ms. Ding: What color do you see in the picture?

Tom: I see the colors of red, blue, yellow, green, purple and brown.

Ms. Ding: Guess! How many color pencils do I need to paint the picture?

Tom: Six color pencils, I guess.

Ms. Ding: No. I only need three color pencils.

Lesson 12 Mixing Colors

Ms. Ding: Mixing colors is interesting. See. Yellow and blue make green. Red and yellow make orange. Red and blue make purple. Have a try!

Amy: Let me try. Oh, yes. The mix of yellow and blue makes green.

Tony: Red and yellow make orange.

Tom: The mix of red and blue makes purple.

Jane: And the mix of white and black makes grey.

All: How interesting it is!

Unit 4 Numbers
Lesson 1 Counting Fun

Ms. Ding: Good morning, boys and girls. Can you count what you see in the room like this?
One little, two little, three little boys.
Four little. five little, six little boys.
Seven little, eight little, nine little boys. Ten little boys in the room.

Isaac: Let me try to sing this song.
One little, two little, three little girls.
Four little, five little, six little girls.
Seven little, eight little, nine little girls.
Ten little girls in the room.

All: Wonderful!

Ms. Ding: Well done. All of you are very good little teachers.

All: Thank you. We are just your pupils.

Ms. Ding: Teachers and pupils learn from each other. Now, let's count the flowers, balls, pencils, dogs, frogs, monkeys and bears in the picture.

All: I can count the flowers. I can count the balls. I can count the dogs. I can count the frogs. I can count the bears. I can count the pencils. I can count the monkeys.

Lesson 2 A Number Rhyme

Ms. Ding: I have a good rhyme about numbers. Do you want to hear it?

All: We do, of course.

Ms. Ding: *One two, take off my shoe.*
Three four, sweep and clean the floor.
Five six, pick up all the sticks.
Seven eight, lay them all straight.
Nine ten, hold a big fat hen.
Eleven twelve, learn, learn and delve.
Do you like this number rhyme?

Steve: Oh, yes. I do. I like this number rhyme very much.

Ms. Ding: Will you please count the shoes and hens in the picture?

Hope: One, two, three, four, five, six, seven, eight, nine, ten, eleven, and twelve. There are twelve hens in all.

James: One, two, three, four, five, six, seven, eight, nine, ten, eleven, and twelve. Twelve shoes in all.

Ms. Ding: Now who wants to count the sticks?

Tom: Let me try. One stick, two sticks, three sticks, four sticks. Oh, too many!

Ms. Ding: Too many to count? Then you may count like this: *One stick, two sticks, three sticks, four. Five sticks, six sticks, seven sticks, more.*

All: One stick, two sticks, three sticks, four. *Five sticks, six sticks, seven sticks, more.*

Ms. Ding: Now let's listen to the number rhyme once again.

Steve: Ok. Let's listen to the rhyme again and see if we can remember it.

Lesson 3 What Time Is It?

Ms. Ding: Now you all can count from 1 to 12, let's learn to tell the time. Now look at the clock. What time is it? It's one. Time, please?

All: It's two. It's three. It's four. It's five. It's six. It's seven. It's eight. It's nine. It's ten. It's eleven. It's twelve.

Ms. Ding: What time is it now, Hope?

Hope: It's six in the morning, time to rise and get ready for school.

Isaac: It's also time to go for a morning run.

Amy: It's six in the evening, time for us girls to go for an evening walk.

Adam: It's also time for me to help clean the house and sweep the floor. What time is it now?

Jane: It's nine in the morning, time to learn English or play house in our English class.

Steve: It's nine in the evening, time for me to go to bed. Time, please?

Tom: It's twelve or noon. It's time to eat. Now it's four in the afternoon, our tea time. I'm very hungry. I want to have some cakes or bread.

Lesson 4 Books on the Desks

Ms. Ding: (Pointing to the desks) Hey guys. Look at your desks. They are not clean.

Steve: Oh, yes. Our desks are not very clean. Let's clean our desks.

Hope: Ok. Let's clean our desks together.

Tom: Good. Oh, one desk, two desks, three desks, four.

All: Five desks, six desks, seven desks, more. Now, our desks are all very clean.

Ms. Ding: Well done. Now everybody: take out your picture book from your backpack, and lay it on your desk.

Helen: Oh, our backpacks are colorful and beautiful.

Ulysses: Where is my English picture book?

Adam: Oh, it is on the floor. There're two books on the floor. Do you love your picture books?

Ulysses: Sure, we do. We love our picture books very much.

Tom: Thank you, Adam. Thanks a lot.

James: Now let me put my paper ships in my clean desk. Look! Here they are! One ship, two ships, three ships, four,

All: Five ships, six ships, seven ships, more.

Ms. Ding: Please say the word "ship" clearly. A ship isn't a sheep. A sheep isn't a ship. Listen carefully, please. *One sheep, two sheep, three sheep, four.*

All: Five sheep, six sheep, seven sheep, more.

Lesson 5 Hats on Heads

Ms. Ding: Wow! You have so many paper hats. Some of them are big and some small. Please put that small hat on your head, Adam.

Adam: Ok. Put the small hat on my head.

Tom: A small hat on a big head. That's funny.

Ms. Ding: Now look at the picture. Who can count the ducks, the cats, and the birds?

Tony: I can count the cats: one, two, three, and four. There are four big cats.

Judy:	I can count the birds. One little, two little, three little birds, four little, five little, six little birds. There are six little birds in the picture.
Steve:	Let me try. I see the two little cats and the two big birds. Their heads are small, but the hats on their heads are big.
Jane:	I can count the little ducks: one, two, three, four, five, six, seven, eight, nine, ten, eleven, and twelve. There're twelve little ducks in all. Their heads are very small.
Ms. Ding:	Good job. Now look at my two hands: left hand and right hand.
Helen:	I see. This is my left hand, and this is my right hand. I have two hands.

Lesson 6 My Two Feet

Ms. Ding:	Every child likes Children's Day.
Steve:	Every child? Am I a child?
Ms. Ding:	Yes, you are. You are a child of your dad and mom. You're the boy and the son of your parents. How many children are there in our class?
All:	One child, two children, three children, and four children, five children, six children, seven children, and more.
Ulysses:	We are all children. We children are smart and bright.
Ms. Ding:	Now, look at the picture. See, there are ten little toes on two feet: right foot, left foot, two feet.
Steve:	I see, one foot, two feet. There are ten little toes on two feet.
Ms. Ding:	Stand up, please. *Left foot, right foot, left foot, right.* *Left foot up, right foot down.* *Up and down, left foot, right.*
All:	*Left foot, right foot, left foot, right.*

	Left foot up, right foot down. *Up and down, left foot, right.*
Ms. Ding:	We walk on our feet.
Steve:	We run on our feet.
Tom:	We jump on our feet.
Hope:	We dance on our feet too.

Lesson 7 Song of One to Twenty

Steve:	Now we can say the numbers from one to twelve. Will you please teach us how to count more numbers, Ms. Ding?
Ms. Ding:	Sure. Let me teach you how to count from one to twenty. I have a song that will help you learn. Here we go. (Singing) *One two three four five six seven eight nine ten (twice). Eleven twelve thirteen fourteen fifteen sixteen. Seventeen eighteen nineteen twenty.*
All:	(Singing)

Lesson 8 Learn How to Count from 1 to 100

Ms. Ding:	Now, let's learn how to count from 1 to 100. Here is a list from 1 to 100. Now look at the list. I'll read the numbers like this. Listen carefully, please... 10、20、30、40、50、60、70、80、90、100. *Who can read the numbers from 20 to 29?*
A:	I can. 20 21 22 23 24 25 26 27 28 29. *Now who can read the numbers from 30 to 39?*
B:	*I can. 30、31、32、33、34、35、36、37、38、39. Who can read the numbers from 40 to 49?*
C:	*Me. I will. 40、41、42、43、44、45、46、47、48、49. Now who can read the numbers from 50 to 59?*
D:	*Let me try. 50、51、52、53、54、55、56、57、58、59. Now who can read the*

numbers from 60 to 69?

E: *Sure, I can. 60、61、62、63、64、65、66、67、68、69. Now who can read the numbers from 70 to 79?*

F: *Let me try. 70、71、72、73、74、75、76、77、78、79. Now who can read the numbers from 80 to 89?*

G: *Let me try. 80、81、82、83、84、85、86、87、88、89. Now who can read the numbers from 90 to 100?*

H: *Let me try. 90、91、92、93、94、95、96、97、98、99、100.*

Ms. Ding: Now each of you picks a line and reads the numbers carefully...

Lesson 9 Lucky Number

Ms. Ding: Come over here, guys. Take a number from this jug. When your number is called and you answer to the call correctly, you will get a piece of candy. So let's say this is your lucky number. Please listen carefully to the number. I start calling 19.

Ulysses: Number 90 is here.

Tom: Number 19 is here. Hey, Ulysses. It is 19 not 90. Do I get a piece of candy?

Ms. Ding: Yes, you do. Now you lead, Tom.

Tom: Cool. 19 is my lucky number. Now I am calling lucky number 66.

Helen: Number 66 is here.

Tom: All right. You also get a piece of candy, Helen.

Lesson 10 A Calling Game

Steve: Each of us has a number card. Please look at the number on your card. This is your number. I have the card of number one. So let me start calling a number. Now let's begin. Number one is calling number 30.

Isaac: Number 30 is calling number 13. Number 30 is calling number 13. Be quick to answer. Who has number 13?

James: Oh, I'm number 13. I'm calling number 33.

Tom: Number 33 is calling number 12.

Eva: Number 2 is calling number 20.

Tom: Wrong. You lose, Eva.

Steve: Eva, you are wrong. No one called number 2.

Ulysses: I am number 12. Number 12 is calling Number 15.

Judy: Number 15 is calling number 50.

Lesson 11 We Love Our Country

Ms. Ding: Look at your paper. It has 100 dots on it. Will you please connect the dots from 1 to 44? This is a map of China. China is our country. Now, connect the dots from 45 to 100. What does the picture show?

Steve: 56 kids are in the map. It means we love our country. It also means the country is us all.

Lesson 12 One World, One Dream

Ms. Ding: It's a picture puzzle. We need to connect the dots from 1 to 100. Can you do that for me? Now, what does the picture show?

All: One world, one dream.

Ms. Ding: Great! One world and one dream. The world is like a big family. Everyone in the family wants to live happily and peacefully. This is the dream of us all.

图书在版编目（CIP）数据

我的第一本英语听说入门书：全 2 册 / 丁洁著 . —北京：北京
联合出版公司，2012.12

ISBN 978-7-5502-1180-3

Ⅰ.①我… Ⅱ.①丁… Ⅲ.①英语－听说教学－儿童教育－教材
Ⅳ.① H319.9

中国版本图书馆 CIP 数据核字（2012）第 278084 号

我的第一本英语听说入门书（1、2）

选题策划： 日知图书

作　　者： 丁　洁
插　　画： 杜晓西
责任编辑： 李　伟
特约编辑： 苟志和
美术编辑： 张鹤飞
封面设计： 垠　子
版式设计： 孙阳阳

北京联合出版公司出版
（北京市西城区德外大街 83 号楼 9 层　100088）
北京缤索印刷有限公司印刷　新华书店经销
字数50千字　787×1092毫米　1／12　18印张
2013年1月第1版　2013年1月第1次印刷
ISBN 978-7-5502-1180-3
定价：120.00元（全2册）
